MW00737659

BOOP-OOP-A-DOOP

· MEANS ·

I LOVE YOU

BOOP-OOP-A-DOOP

· MEANS ·

I LOVE YOU

Andrews McMeel
Publishing

Kansas City

Boop-Oop-A-Doop Means I Love You

© 2003 King Features Syndicate, Inc. / Fleischer Studios, Inc.™ Hearst Holdings, Inc. / Fleischer Studios, Inc. All rights reserved. Printed in China. No part of this book may be used or reproduced in any manner whatsoever without written permission except in the case of reprints in the context of reviews. For information, write Andrews McMeel Publishing, an Andrews McMeel Universal company, 4520 Main Street, Kansas City, Missouri 64111.

ISBN: 0-7407-3844-5

Library of Congress Control Number: 2003102254

03 04 05 06 07 WKT 10 9 8 7 6 5 4 3 2 1

Written by Patrick Regan
Book design and composition by Judith Stagnitto Abbate / Abbate Design

BOOP-OOP-A-DOOP

• MEANS •

I LOVE YOU

Love's a tune
that's always
thrilling...

a SWEET DESSERT
that's never filling.

Love will sweep your blues away.

Love will keep
you on your toes.

Love can cure
your deepest woes.

Love is such a
GROOVY thing...

And when your spirits start to droop . . .

love brings back your
Boop-Oop-A-Doop!

Love's the tastiest confection.

Love is good for
your complexion.

Love feels like a CELEBRATION...

it's BETTER than a
beach vacation.

Love is grandé.
Love's a kick.

Love's a treat
without the trick.

Love can make a
grown girl giggle...

and turn your WALK
into a WIGGLE.

Love will make your toe tips tingle . . .

and make you glad
that you're not single.

With love, you're always in the loop.

So let it loose—
don't be a poop.

Love can speak with just a wink.

It says a MOUTHFUL, don't you think?

Love's demure.

Love will raise your temperature.

Love's CONTAGIOUS.

Love's a DARE.

Love can catch
you unaware.

Love is wild.
Love's FEROCIOUS.

Without it, life would be atrocious!

So when you wish

upon a star. . .

DON'T wish for money, jewels, or cars.

You'll feel as rich as J. Paul Getty...

**if you listen close
to darling Betty.**

'Cause LOVE is all you really need . . .

to make you feel

quite rich indeed.